T0199032

PAMELA WOLF

The Old Testament Poem Book

WestBow Press books may be ordered through booksellers or by contacting:

WestBow Press
A Division of Thomas Nelson & Zondervan
1663 Liberty Drive
Bloomington, IN 47403
www.westbowpress.com
1 (866) 928-1240

ISBN: 978-1-9736-9323-9 (sc)
ISBN: 978-1-9736-9324-6 (e)

Library of Congress Control Number: 2020910425

Print information available on the last page.

WestBow Press rev. date: 06/10/2020

WestBow
PRESS®
A DIVISION OF THOMAS NELSON
& ZONDERVAN

CREATION

Jeremiah 10:12; Colossians 1:15-17; Genesis 1:1-10; Genesis 1:11-25; 2:8, 9 Psalm 83:18; Genesis 1:26-31; 2:7-25 Genesis 2:16, 17; 3:1-13, 24; Revelation 12:9 Genesis 3:16-23; 2; Revelation 21:3, 4

Our God made lots of angels and he also made the wondrous earth
    It brought a lot of water and it gave a lot of plants their birth
Then God made stars for nighttime and he also made the sun for day
    It brought a place called Eden where a lot of creatures made their way
Then God made dust a man and named him Adam as he gave him life
    It brought him lots of loneliness so God made Eve to be his wife
Then God forbid a fruit tree that could only make the couple die
    It brought a snake to tempt them and they took two bites that made them cry
Then God asked both of them to leave and live with thistles and a thorn
    It brought a lot of hardships and the perfect life they had was torn
Then God began to teach them not to disobey the words he said
    It brought a lot of lessons and he gave them children in their bed

CAIN AND ABEL

Genesis 4:2-26; 1 John 3:11, 12; John 11:25

The first two humans children started out with Abel after Cain
　　Cain farmed a lot and acted bad to give his brother lots of pain
So God loved Abel better and the way he herded lots of sheep
　　Sheep loved him more than Cain and so his jealousy began to weep
So Abel got a rock and killed his brother at that fateful time
　　Time quickly passed till God would send him off to live without a dime
So if you kill your brother than the lord is gonna send you out
　　Out in to a land where there's no water from a running spout

GIANTS IN THE EARTH

Genesis 6:1-8; Jude 6

That man named Cain was an awful man like Satan who was in the sky
    and he was born an angel but he used his life to steal and lie
So he sent other angels down as all their human bodies formed
    and then each one could marry with the honey from the bees that swarmed
So then each one was happy as their children grew to be so tall
    and then the giants used their strength for things that God would never call
So then the world was awful as they made a lot of people bad
    and God made plans to change things as he sat there feeling dazed and sad

NOAH'S ARK

Genesis 6:9-22; 7:1-9 Genesis 7:10-24; 8:1-17; Peter 3:19, 20 Genesis 8:18-22; 9:9-17

The world's good people rested stark and God made plans to flood the earth
    Then God made Noah build an ark and that took years to give it birth
Then Noah warned the people there and all the people laughed at him
    Then creatures came beneath his care and filled the ark above it's brim
Then Noah and his family slept and rain fell down for forty days
    Then evil people died and wept and Noah's family gave him praise
Then Noah's dove went out to look and brought them back an olive leaf
    Then rainbows shone above the brook and took away the family's grief

THE TOWER OF BABEL

Genesis 10:1, 8-10; 11:1-9

Some years since Noah's flood had passed and Noah's family grew and grew
    and then a man named Nimrod told a lot of people what to do
And he had made himself a king and built a tower towards the sky
    and did it so the people would be underneath the place he'd lie
And God made different languages to make them leave the tower there
    and have them live around the world with lot's of types of food to share
And people liked that better and they started looking different too
    and all the different people started making all the world so new

ABRAHAM

Genesis 11:27-32; 12:1-7; 17:1-8, 15-17; 18:9-19 Genesis 21:1-7; 22:1-18

When God put folks around the world a man named Abraham was there
    and Abraham was someone who was always kind and acted fair
So God was friends with Abraham and chose him as a man to teach
    and Abraham went walking with his family cross the land to preach
So God was feeling happy and gave Abraham a newborn son
    and Abraham was ancient with a miracle he'd truly won
So God began to test him and tell Abraham to kill his child
    and Abraham was loyal as he walked up mountains through the wild
So God told Abraham to stop and never harm that special boy
    and Abraham and Sarah kept their Isaac that was full of joy

LOT'S WIFE LOOKED BACK

Genesis 13;5-13; 18:20-33; 19:1-29; Luke 17:28-32; 2 Peter 2:6-8

The years went by and Isaac's cousin lot was living with his herds
    and herds from uncle Abraham were making such a crowded place
The place that uncle Abraham began to give him bitter words
    and words about them spreading out for room to let the creatures race
The race moved Lot to Sodom with his children and his pretty, wife
    and then his wife began to see that people there were acting mean
The mean and evil people gave the family such an awful, life
    and life was full of angels that came down to try to stop the scene
The scene was when the angels told them not to look back as they'd leave
    and leave as God destroyed that awful city that was full of fault
The fault was made when Lot's wife looked right back as turns began to weave
    and weave her body up in to a pillar that was made of salt

ISAAC GETS MARRIED

Genesis 24:1-67

The days were sad as Isaac grieved to hear his mother Sarah died
    and he began to see his father want to help him get a bride
And then he sent his servant to Haran and he was near the well
    and he began to pray to find a women that was sweet to tell
And then a women helped him feed his camels which was such a fight
    and he began to ask her if the group of them could spend the night
And then the women's father said that she could go to marry him
    and he began to take the happy women off as skies went dim

ISAAC AND REBEKAH'S CHILDREN

Genesis 25:5-11, 020-34, 35; 27:1-46; 28:1-5; Hebrew 12:16, 17

When Isaac and Rebekah met they knew their love was meant to last
    And then when they were married off they got two twins that grew up fast
And Isaac showed his Esau love much more cause he would hunt him food
    And Jacob won his mother's heart with all his love and peaceful mood
And then when Esau married both his women didn't love the lord
    And Jacob got his blessings first so Esau went to get a sword
And then their mother worried so she made her love named Jacob leave
    And sent him to Haran to find his uncle for a wife that eve

JACOB IN HARAN WITH UNCLE LABAN

Genesis 29:1-30

Haran was far away so Jacob found the well to get a drink
    and then he asked two men if they could find his uncle cross the brink
And then his uncle's daughter Rachel came to him and got a kiss
    and then he told her why he'd come and she was in a state of bliss
And then his uncle said he had to earn her with the fields for years
    and then when seven passed his uncle changed his mind which brought them tears
And then he offered Leah cause his Jacob always stayed so true
    and then when lot's more years had passed he let him marry Rachel too

JACOB'S ENORMOUS FAMILY

Genesis 29:32-35; 30:1-26; 35:16-19; 37:35

When Jacob married Rachel she had little luck in giving birth
    but Leah gave him children and she took away the barren mirth
And both the wives gave servants to their husband so they'd birth much more
    but then his Rachel had a son named Joseph that they'd all adore
And those were the eleven sons that Jacob had when he was there
    but then he had some daughters too and they were given lot's of care
And Jacob missed his home so they sought Canaan with their hefty, herds
    but it was sad cause Rachel's birth began to give her deathly words
And then those children made the nation's population start to fill
    but it would never cease to have more room for those with Dinah's will

JACOB'S DAUGHTER DINAH

Genesis 34:1-31

That Jacob's daughter Dinah friended women from the Canaan land
    a land where people worshiped lot's of false Gods on the temple's sand
And that made Jacob angry as a man named She' chem made her lie
    and lie upon the earth to get some pleasure as he made her cry
Then Dinah's brothers killed him in that city with a single sword
    a sword that made their father Jacob scream at them in quite a cord

JACOB'S FAVORITE SON JOSEPH

Genesis 37:1-35 Genesis 39:1-23; 40:1-23 Genesis 41:1-57; 42:1-8; 50:20 Genesis 42:9-38; 43:1-34; 44:1-34 Genesis 45:1-28; 46:1-27

That man named Jacob loved his favorite, son dear Joseph very, much
  and then dear Joseph got a long, striped, coat that felt so good to touch
Then his brothers got so jealous so they threw dear Joseph down a hole
  and then they got some silver as they sold dear Joseph just like coal
Then all of them began to bloody up the coat dear Joseph wore
  and then they showed their father as dear Joseph found a servant's door
Then their dear Joseph worked so hard and took good charge of all the house
  and then dear Joseph saw his master's wife as such an awful, spouse
Then she tried to get dear Joseph to commit a sin and lie with her
  and then dear Joseph wouldn't bend as plans of spite began to stir
Then Pharaoh's wife was saying that dear Joseph was the one to blame
  and then dear Joseph found a prison cell that he had come to claim
Then prisoners began to tell dear Joseph when they had their dreams
  and then dear Joseph told them what they meant beneath the window's beams
Then pharaoh asked dear Joseph about dreams where grains ate smaller grains
  and then he told dear Joseph that the dreams had cows that ate their strains
Then sweet dear Joseph told him that a famine would be coming there
  and then he chose dear Joseph to collect them food to save and share
Then eight years later famine came that made dear Joseph feel so sad
  and then dear Joseph saw his brothers come to get the food he had
Then none of them could recognize dear Joseph under Egypt's skies
  and then dear Joseph recognized his brothers but he called them spies

Then Simon was asked to stay as their dear Joseph made his other brothers go
    and then dear Joseph saw them come right back with empty sacks to show
Then servants filled their bags as their dear Joseph filled a silver, cup
    and then dear Joseph told the maids to look for them and catch right up
Then Benjamin was ceized as their dear Joseph said he had to stay
    and then Judah told dear Joseph that he'd take his brother's place that day
Then Judah told dear Joseph that their Benjamin was Jacob's grace
    and then dear Joseph knew they'd changed and put a smile upon his face
Then he revealed himself as their dear Joseph who was Egypt's king
    and then dear Joseph took them all to live with them beneath his wing

JOB

Job 1:1-22: 2:1-13; 42:10-17

A man named Job was a faithful man so Satan took away his sheep
They died as fast as cattle ran which made good Job begin to weep
The tears began to make a storm that robbed Job of his children's lives
Then lot's of illness came to form and Job was given burning hives
But Job was still a faithful, man so God brought back a lot of sheep
They lived as long as cattle ran which made good job begin to weep
The tears began to make a storm that brought Job back his children's lives
Then lot's of wellness came to form and healed Job of his burning hives
So always keep your faith in God like Job who had eternal life
That brought good Job to Jesse's rod who lived in Eden with his wife

MOSES SAVES THE ISRAELITES

Exodus 1:6-22; Exodus 2:1-10; Exodus 2:11-25; Acts 7;22-29; Exodus 3;1-22; 4;1-20;
Exodus 4:27-31: 5;1-23: 6;1-13; 26-30; 7:1-13; Exodus chapters 7 to 12; Exodus chapters
12 to 15

King Joseph died and the brand new pharaoh made the Israelites his slaves
They were whipped as they grew which made the pharaoh fear that they'd gain strength in waves
So the pharaoh told the midwives to begin to kill each newborn boy
But they wouldn't so the pharaoh told his soldiars to start killing joy
That made a mother hide her baby Moses from the pharaoh's wrath
Then she put him in a basket as the river graced the pharaoh's path
It happened as his sister watched and the pharaoh's daughter found him there
Then the pharaoh's daughter called to get an Israelite who'd give him care
So Moses's mother nursed him till the pharaoh's daughter took him in
But he always knew just who he was as the pharaoh went about his sin
Then one day when he'd grown up Moses went and saw what pharaoh did
That made him kill a man as pharaoh chased him and he went and hid
It took him from the pharaoh to a sheperd's life for fourty years
Then he saw a burning bush that made him think of pharaoh and his fears
It brought God's voice that told him to go free the slaves from pharoah's hand
But Moses feared that pharaoh wouldn't buy his tale in Egypt's land
So God told him to throw a stick that would be a snake at pharaoh's feet
That's what he did and the pharoah wouldn't budge each time that they would meet
Then God made plagues until the pharoah let the slaves in Egypt leave
It made the pharoah angry as the loaded carts began to weave
So the pharoah sent his gaurds as God made clouds so that they couldn't see
Then the pharoah lost as Moses parted waters which would set them free

LIFE WITH THE LEAD OF MOSES

Exodus 16:1-36; Numbers 11:7-9; Joshua 5:10-12 Exodus 19:1-25; 20:1-21: 24:12-18;
31:18; Deuteronomy 6:4-6; Leviticus 19:18 Matthew 22:36-40 Exodus 32:1-35

The Israelites in Canaan didn't see God give a lot to eat
So God rained down some thin, white cakes that tasted very soft and sweet
It fed them for so many years as Moses showed God such a lead
Then he heard God call him up the mount to hear commandments that they'd need
So Moses told the Israelites to only ever worship God
It made the mountains smoke as God made thunder blast with every odd
Then God called Moses back to get two flat, stones with some written laws
So Moses stayed for fourty days to learn how God could make pain pause
That made them start to wonder where their lead and God had gone and been
Then they made a golden, calf their God to worship which indeed was sin
So Moses and God angered when he came back and he got his sword
It killed three thousand Israelites who hadn't kept their God a lord
The story tells how much the Israelites should not have strayed from God
Cause God knows all and when they disobeyed he killed them with his rod

THE TABERNACLE

Exodus 25:8-40; 26:1-37; 27:1-8; 28:1;30:1-10, 17-21; 34:1, 2; Hebrews 9:1-5

God told the faithful Israelites to build a tabernacle there
    And they chopped a lot of wood and made some fabric as a tent for prayer
Then it had a box with angels that contained commandments on two rocks
    And it made the Israelites go in for prayer in very massive flocks
Then the priests led worship near the jar of manna and thwelve loaves of bread
    And it sat right by the lamp stand that had seven lamps as prayer was said
Then they sacrificed dead animals by burning them right near their bowl
    And the priests began to wash themselves and prayer began to cleanse each soul
Then the Israelites packed up the tabernacle and they walked through woods
    And the wilderness heard lot's of prayer as Israelites moved all their goods
Then they felt so glad no matter where they were or how their time was spent
    And they always loved to worship while each prayer was said inside their tent
Then the lord made up a law that everyone should worship in one place
    And the prayer was given lots more strength as songs of love showed God's bright face

THE THWELVE SPIES

Numbers 13:1-33; 14:1-38

The Israelites always wandered through the wilderness in search of fruit
Then the Israelites found Canaan as their leader Moses showed the route
It made him send thwelve Israelites who spied some fruit inside the land
But the people there were big as the Israelites told Moses at his hand
So the Israelites were scared that all the fruit would come to bring a war
Then they wanted rid of Moses to protect the Israelites much more
But two spies calmed the Israelites to get some rods of fruit to eat
It made the Israelites begin to want the spies and Moses beat
So God was mad about thoughts that the Israelites began to think
Then God let spies of Israelites and Moses go to get a drink
But the other Israelites stayed there and wandered wilderness for years
And the story praises Israelites who always looked at God with fears

AARON'S ROD

Numbers 16:1-49; 17:1-11; 26:10

The Israelites didn't think that brother Aaron should remain the priest
 And they didn't think that Moses should be leading them to say the least
So Moses told them all to put some incense in fire holders there
 And they graced the tabernacle where the lord would tell his choice with care
Then the grounds began to open up to swallow those who did them wrong
 And a fire burned their clothes as others ran much faster than a song
Then God told Moses to tell the leaders of each tribe to bring their rods
 And they put them in the tent to hear his choice of who should lead all odds
That made a lot of flowers grow on Aaron's rod to show the choice
 And Aaron was a good high priest who soothed so many with his voice
So Aaron led them till he'd died when he had gotten very old
 And they knew that God had chosen him since he was very kind and bold

THE SNAKES

Numbers 21:4-9; John 3:14, 15

The Israelites complained to God cause there was little food or drink
    And they were tired of manna that they'd had for longer than a blink
So God was mad about the sin that didn't have a thankful way
    And then God sent down snakes that killed so many when they came to stay
Then Israelites asked Moses if he'd pray to God to find a cure
    And he was told to make a copper snake to put new life in store
That made God kill the beasts when they all saw the snake upon the pole
    And that put lot's of happiness inside of every single soul
It taught the Israelites to give their thanks to God no matter what
    And they did that forever more which made the doors of troubles shut

A NEW LEADER

Numbers 21:21-35; 22:1-40; 23:1-30; 24:1-25 27:12-23; Deuteronomy 3:23-29; 31:1-8, 14-23; 32:45-52; 34:1-12

The king of Canaan feared that all the Israelites were very strong
So he payed a man named Balaam to go curse them which indeed was wrong
Then he rode away from Canaan on his donkey that kept trying to turn
And the donkey sat as he saw the brightest angel like a golden urn
So Balaam beat the donkey right near Canaan as it came to speak
Then the creature asked him why he'd started beating him to make him weak
That made the angel right near Canaan show himself to Balaam there
And God said not to curse the Israelites but treat them with his care
So Balaam blessed them all as Moses planned to enter Canaan soon
But God was mad about the past and picked a new lead by the moon
Then Joshua showed them Canaan as their former leader got so old
That made him die and everyone was sad as Moses lay there cold
But Joshua was good to them and Canaan was a perfect place
So God's plan always led them and it always came to bring them grace

GOING IN TO CANAAN

Joshua 2:1-24; Hebrews 11:31 Joshua 3:1-17; 4:1-18 Joshua 6:1-25

The Israelites were ready to go in to Canaan on that day
    So Joshua sent two spies who found a women's house that let them stay
But someone saw the Israelites and told the king that there were spies
    So they hid out on the roof as gaurds went there to get them with their cries
Then she said that the Israelites were gone as the gaurds went looking for the two
    So they were saved as the women asked them for a favor that they'd do
And it was a request to spare her family when the Israelites came
    So they gave her a cord to dangle from the window that was red like flame
Then God told the Israelites to cross the river as it dried right up
    So walking there was easy as they carried every golden cup
It made the Israelites feel glad to walk around the city walls
    So when they went to war it brought a lot of horns and happy calls
Then God took down the walls as the Israelites burned every house that night
    So all was gone except for where the women lived who'd done them right

THE THIEF

Joshua 7:1-26; 8:1-29

Joshua sent some men to fight a city that was known as A'i
Then the men were killed or ran away as he was sad and asked God why
That told the leader Joshua that someone had commited sin
Then God told him to kill the man in order to make armies win
So Joshua gathered every man and he picked out the guilty one
Then the man admitted that he'd stolen goods that shone just like the sun
Those things were found inside his tent and Joshua dug them from the dirt
Then the man was stoned to death with all his family which indeed did hurt
That made the men of Joshua start winning lot's of battles more
So then they were taught a lesson about sin and what it put in store

THE GIBEONITES

Joshua 9:1-27; 10:1-5 Joshua 10:6-15; 12:7-24; 14:1-5; Judge 2:8-13

The cities in Canaan got prepared for when the Israelites would come
But the city of Gibeon felt afraid that they would lose and all look dumb
So they put on ragged clothes and loaded donkeys like they'd traveled far
Then they said that they had heard of him since miracles made him a star
So they offered to be servants if he promised not to fight their clan
But Joshua found that they lived close since he was such a brilliant man
Then he promised not to kill them as he took them underneath his wing
That peace made them the servants but it also angered up the king
So he brought a group to battle the Gibeonites which gave them lot's of fear
Then Joshua came to help as God dropped loads of massive hailstorms near
It killed some as he prayed that God would not retire the glowing sun
That made it stay until the men of Joshua had truly won
Then Joshua spent a lot of years in battles till the day he died
It payed off since it filled the Israelites with every ounce of pride

DEBORAH THE PROPHETESS

Jugdes 2:14-22; 4:1-24; 5:1-31

Deborah was a prophetess and she also served them as a judge
So the Israelites would go to get her help when troubles wouldn't budge
Then Deborah the prophetess told the judge Barak about a war
So the Israelites knew that it was time to fight the king of Canaan more
It brought the prophetess Deborah to mount Tabor with the army men
So the Israelites knew that it was time to make that mount a lion's den
Then the prophetess Deborah watched God bring a flood that fell down from the sky
So the Israelites saw their leader run away as many came to die
Then dreams of the prophetess Deborah came as their leader ran in to a tent
So the Israelites knew that he would drink some milk and fall asleep while pent
Then the prophetess Deborah told them that a tent pin would go through his head
So the Israelites knew that they had won cause all the soldiars wound up dead
That means that the prophetess Deborah saved them since she listened to the lord
So the Israelites had great success each time that they picked up a sword

RUTH, NAOMI AND ORPAH

The book of Ruth

Naomi and her family walked from Israel in search of food
    Then her spouse and two sons went with her to Moab where they all stayed glued
It was happy till Naomi's husband died which left her cold as stone
    Then her two sons married Ruth and Orpah when the two of them were grown
That followed with the two sons death as Naomi made her plans to leave
    Then the two girls came along as roads to Israel began to weave
But Naomi said that they'd be better off if they went on their way
    Then Orpah left as Ruth refused so she gave up and let her stay
That brought Ruth and Naomi in to Israel so very fast
    Then they met a man named Boaz who made lot's of happy memories last
It got Ruth married quickly and Naomi's spirits came to rise
    Then they knew that God had seen Ruth's love and sent her giant heart a prize

JUDGE GIDEON

Judges chapters 6 to 8

The Israelites were under strength of Midian which felt so bad
So they asked the lord for help when they were hit and kicked as they felt sad
Then he told judge Gideon to make the Israelites in to an army group
So 32,000 men began to serve the lord inside in their coup
But God felt that the Israelites had made the army way too large
And the lord did not want them to think that they had won without his charge
So God then told judge Gideon to send scared Israelites from there
But after that the lord still felt that way too many came to bare
So he told judge Gideon to bring the Israelites to drink down by the stream
Then the lord chose all who kept watch as they drank beneath the sun's bright beam
So the Israelites who drank with hands went down to where the others slept
It served the lord as they blew horns and broke jars with the cries they wept
Then the Israelites began to win since they had really done the tasks
That shows how much the lord will give if people do the things he asks

THE PROMISE OF JEPHTHAH

Judges 10:6-18; 11:1-40

The Israelites stopped loving God so the land of Am'mon made them hurt
    Then they asked for help as a lot of them bent down to pray upon the dirt
So God forgave the Israelites and picked judge Jephthah for the fight
    Then he promised God the first to greet him home if victory came that night
That gave the Israelites sucess and his daughter came to greet him home
    Then they knew a tabernacle was the place where she would always roam
It made the Israelites feel sad cause she would have to leave her friends
    Then she told her father that he'd made a promise that should stay till ends
So she lived at Shiloh where the Israelites came visiting each year
    Then they knew that they had climbed to go and bring a faithful servant near

JUDGE SAMSON

Judges chapters 13 to 16

Judge Samson was the strongest and he killed a lion with his hands
Those hands doomed lot's of philistines who lived upon the Canaan lands
Then Samson fell in love with his Delilah who was very sweet
But sweet days left when philistines began to want this strong man beat
So they told Delilah that that they'd give her silver if she helped them out
Then out she went to get her Samson's secret with her pretty pout
That told her that his long locks were a gift from God to give him strength
That strength would leave when Samson slept and she cut off his locks with length
Then the philistines made him their slave and also took his big brown eyes
Those eyes were gone but Samson's hair grew back which made his muscles rise
So he had a servant lead him to a pillar at a party place
That place was where they laughed at Samson as they threw things at his face
So he prayed to God for strength as pillars broke and ceilings came to fall
That fall came down on Samson and the philistines which killed them all
So then he beat the philistines since he had kept his faith in God
And God brought Samson up to be in heaven with his ruling rod

THE STORY OF SAMUEL

1 Samuel 1:1-28; 2:11-36; 4:16-18; 8:4-9

Hannah couldn't have a child so she began to kneel and pray
  Then she said the son would find a tabernacle where he'd always stay
So Hannah and her husband went to visit their child every year
  Then they brought their son a sleeveless coat each time as Samuel looked so dear
So the high priest's two boys tried to make the child do lot's of awful things
  Then the son ignored them both as Samuel stayed as ethical as kings
So then as the child went down to sleep he heard somebody call his name
  Then the son went to the priest who said his voice was not the one to claim
So the child went back to bed where someone called his name a second time
  Then he went back to the priest who told that son the same thing like a rhyme
So then as it came again the priest knew God had come to call the child
  Then the son named Samuel answered him and got some news that sounded wild
So the child knew that the boys would die in battle and so very soon
  Then the priest who lost each son fell down and broke his neck beneath the moon
So then he was dead as the child named Samuel took his place so very fast
  Then the son knew that the punishments were just as he made goodness last

SAUL

1 Samuel chapters 9 to 11; 13:5-14; 14:47-52; 15:1-35; 2 Samuel 1:23

God told Samuel to pour some oil on Saul's head to make him the king
A king that acted humble as he flew much faster than a wing
So Saul won lot's of battles as he stood tall with a handsome face
That face loved his son Jonathon who always helped him win with grace
Then Saul heard that the philistines were coming for another war
A war that made the priest named Samuel want a sacrifice in store
But he told Saul to wait until he'd come back which was taking long
A long time passed so he went on and did it which was very wrong
Then Samuel came and told Saul that he'd disobeyed him very much
So much of that went on until his crown was not a thing he'd touch
That shows that king Saul shouldn't have gone on to stray from faithful ways
Those ways are always faithful since they give the lord above such praise

SAMUEL CHOOSES DAVID

1 Samuel 17:34, 16:1-13 1 Samuel 17:1-54

Samuel heard God tell him to find Jesse's house and choose a son
Then God said that the boy would be a king and Israel's chosen one
So Samuel followed God as Jesse brought his groups of children near
But God just didn't want to choose them since he didn't find them dear
Then David came and God knew that this boy would be a perfect choice
Cause God knew that he loved his father's sheep and had a gentle voice
So God told Samuel to pour some oil on David's head to raise him up
Then David followed God in to a palace with each silver cup
That brought his oldest brothers to the army where they made God proud
Then the Philistines came back as God looked down and saw them being loud
The noise came from a giant that was teasing God and all the men
They heard him tell God that he'd go and stab them like a fish or hen
So David got some stones as God stood by him as to make him strong
That hit the giant and he died as God's will took away each wrong

DAVID RUNNING AWAY

1 Samuel 18:1-300 19:1-18 1 Samuel 22:1-4; 25:1-43

David was an army chief and lived inside the royal house
It made king Saul feel jelous cause he felt much smaller than a mouse
So he threw spears at David but he moved which always made him miss
Then Saul took back the promise that his daughter would give him a kiss
That followed with him telling David that they'd marry if he killed
So Saul watched lot's of Philistines go down as all their blood was spilled
Then David married her which didn't stop the throwing of the spears
It brought the men of Saul as he went out to hide for many years
The time was spent in caves and David had his family live with him
He'd run from Saul and then become a leader as the skies went dim
Then David asked a man if he could share his many goats and sheep
But he was mean like Saul and said he'd kill them as he came to weep
So David left as the mean man's wife convinced him not to kill them all
Then she brought some food as they lived a life of happiness and free of Saul
That followed with the mean man's death as David took her as a wife
So since he didn't give up he lost Saul and had a happy life

DAVID IS KING

1 Samuel 26:1-25; 27:1-7; 31:1-6; 2 Samuel 1:26; 3:1-21; 5:1-10; 1 Chronicles 11:1-9 2 Samuel 11:1-27; 12:1-18 1 Kings 1:1-48

David learned that Saul was trying to capture him and sent some spies
They found out where the army camp was sleeping underneath the skies
So David and his nephew stole the spear of Saul and water jug
Then they left the army camp to climb a hill and shout to wake each bug
That told Saul that his things were gone with David who gave out a yell
Then he told the army camp that he would help them win their tale to tell
So David won the battle as he went to Hebron free of Saul
But another army camp came in to to find a king to rule them all
Then David won and Saul was gone as he ruled Hebron seven years
It brought his army camp in to Jerusalem as folks felt fears
That made him king as David felt as powerful as Saul had been
But even when the army camp was gone he still commited sin
So David sinned like Saul and got a married women pregnant there
Then he called the army camp to have the husband killed in battle air
That made God mad much more than any time that Saul and David lied
So troubles riddled him and every army camp until he died

KING SOLOMON IS WISE

1 Kings 3:3-28; 4:29-34

King Solomon was ruler when his father David left the earth
It made God glad to know this teen was giving Israel new birth
So he went to see king Solomon when he was sleeping in a dream
Then God asked him what he would like to make his brand new life there beam
That made him think as good king Solomon asked him for some wisdom there
So God gave out the wisdom that would give Jerusalem such care
Then two women saw king Solomon since they were getting in a fight
It started when God saw them both give birth to baby boys one night
Then soon one died which replaced the live one as king Solomon had slept
So God saw the women wake up with a dead child as she truly wept
Then the other lied about it so they saw king Solomon to pray
It brought God as the king told them to cut the babe in half that day
Then one told good king Solomon to stop it and give him to her
But the other said that God should kill the baby and make bloodshed stir
It told king Solomon that the first young women was the honest one
So God was pleased that Israel was being ruled by David's son

THE BUILDING OF THE TEMPLE

1 chronicles 28:9-21; 29:1-9; 1 kings 5:1-18; 2 chronicles 6:12-42; 7:1-5; 1 kings 11:9-13; 1 kings 11:26-43; 12:1-33; 14:21-31

King Solomon had a ton of men build up a temple made of gold
    And they formed a celebration as his prayer is what the lord was told
It asked the skies above to always listen to the people there
    And a fire came down and burned the sacrifices as light filled the air
It made the people worship in the temple almost every day
    And the king wed lot's of girls who worshiped idols which made madness stay
That got him mean as a prophet spoke to a man there doing building work
    And he said that the kingdom wouldn't stay the king's since he didn't give a perk
So he gave ten tribes to the builder and left two for Solomon's young son
    And the king walked towards the builder as to kill him and he went to run
That followed with the king's death as his son took on and acted mean
    And they had the builder rule a lot of tribes which made their valleys green
But the tribes of Jeroboam worshiped golden idols all the time
    And it all came down to fill the holy city with a load of crime

JEZEBEL AND AHAB

1 kings 16:29-33; 18:-4; 21:1-16; 2 kings 9:30-37

Jeroboam died and almost every king of tribes was very bad
The worst was king Ahab who's wife named Jezebel made people sad
Then they ignored the king and worshiped false gods as she came to kill
That got the king a vineyard as the prophets died to soothe his will
So God sent out some men to where the king and Jezebel would stay
Then she called the king and put on lot's of makeup as she kneeled to pray
But the king was gone and they threw her out the window as she fell and died
So the king was taught a lesson as he lost his wife and sense of pride

GOOD KING JEHOSHAPHAT

1 kings 22:41-53; 2 chronicles 20:1-30

Jehoshaphat was a good king of a two tribe kingdom in the land
The land had such a good life where Jehoshaphat would lend his hand
So things were good until the king Jehoshaphat got awful news
The news was good for armies that would bring Jehoshaphat the blues
Then king Jehoshaphat was good and found Jerusalem for prayer
The prayer was in a temple as Jehoshaphat took good kin there
That brought God's servant as good king Jehoshaphat heard not to fear
The fear was gone as good Jehoshaphat brought both his two tribes near
Then king Jehoshaphat put his good singers in to lead a march
The march sang praise as good Jehoshaphat was strong just like an arch
It took good king Jehoshaphat to where the armies lay there dead
The dead men fought each other good as Jehoshaphat had never bled
That was done by God cause the king Jehoshaphat was good and kept his trust
The trust was strong enough that good Jehoshaphat turned cares to dust

ELISHA AND ELIJAH

1 kings 17:8-24; 2 kings 4:8-37 2 kings 5:1-27

A little boy got sick and died so a prophet took him towards the bed
Then that prophet named Elijah put his hands upon the young boy's head
It brought prayer as the prophet's hands began to bring him back to life
Then that prayer took the prophet Elijah towards his mother which would take his strife
So the prophet's healing partner named Elisha felt so very glad
And the prophet Elijah brought Elisha towards another who was sad
That made the mother happy as the prophets gave her son right back
Then a man who wasn't happy came to the prophet Elijah with a sack
It brought the prophets towards the river where they washed his sore flesh clean
Then the prophet Elijah cured his leprosy on flesh that felt so mean
So the prophets told the future when they cured the people that had died
Then the prophets told about a man who'd always fill them up with pride

JONAH AND THE WHALE

The book of Jonah

That Jonah was a prophet but he didn't do what he was told
So when God sent him to go to Nineveh he ran and bared the cold
Then the prophet Jonah found a boat where lot's of sailors came to form
So when God saw this the skies began to open and release a storm
Then the prophet Jonah told the men to throw him out and make it leave
So when God saw this it calmed and all the sailors left him there to grieve
Then the prophet Jonah was swallowed by a whale and stayed for three whole days
So when God looked down he looked up and apologized with voughts of praise
Then the prophet Jonah was spit up on the land as he was feeling weak
So when God forgave the man he got his strength back and went out to speak

ISAIAH TELLS OF PARADISE

Isaiah 11:6-9; Revelation 21:3, 4

The prophet Isaiah told the world about the paradise to come
And he said that all the flowers would be sweeter than a juicy plum
Then the prophet Isaiah told about the peace between the wolves and sheep
And he said that paradise had waterfalls that always came to weep
Then the prophet Isaiah told that baby calves and lions ate as one
And he said that snakes would never bite beneath the warm and glowing sun
Then the prophet Isaiah told that everyone who followed God would stay
And he said that paradise would come to all of those who kneeled to pray

KING HEZEKIAH

2 Kings 18:1-36; 19:1-37; 21:1-25

Hezekiah ruled the southern two tribes and he felt a lot of stress
That's because Assyrian armies killed the northern tribes and left a mess
Then Hezekiah heard that they would fight his tribes and got some letters too
They were from Assyria and teased his tribes which made him start to stew
So Hezekiah prayed and the prophet Isaiah said that his tribes wouldn't die
Then an angel killed Assyrian tribes as a brand new peace was in the sky
So Hezekiah and his tribes were saved since he had faith and acted good
It would always give the tribes more luck in every single place they stood

KING JOSIAH

2 Chronicles 34:1-28

A lot of kings were bad for years till Josiah ruled when he was eight
The boy would follow good kings so the southern two tribes felt so great
Then as a teen Josiah heard that golden idols served as kings
So as king of kings he broke a lot of statues that wore diamond rings
It followed with Josiah making three men kings of getting cash
Then the kings got large donations and repaired the temple in a flash
That found a book of laws to make Josiah and all kings act kind
But the book was gone for years so kings had never kept those laws in mind
So the king of kings Josiah told his high priest to walk in to town
Then a prophetess said that kings would go through lives that always made them frown
It would happen to the kings for years when good Josiah wound up dead
So the king of kings told a man named Jeremiah to inform each head
Then he served as a prophet as kings unlike Josiah only laughed at him
But he kept on telling kings and crowds that idols made the future dim
That's what he told the kings for years until Josiah finally died
Then the kings had an example of a ruler that could bring them pride

THE BOYS IN BABYLON

Daniel 1:1-21

King Nebuchadnezzar of Babylon fought Jerusalem and won the fight
Then Nebuchadnezzar took the smartest as his servants on that night
That brought them back to Babylon as Nebuchadnezzar chose some boys
They were smart and cute so Nebuchadnezzar trained them to bring palace joys
It went on for years as Nebuchadnezzar gave the boys good food and wine
Then one told king Nebuchadnezzar that some vegetables would serve them fine
That showed king Nebuchadnezzar that he looked as good when ten days passed
So Nebuchadnezzar came to choose him and his three friends very fast
Then Nebuchadnezzar had them help with choices since they acted wise
And Nebuchadnezzar knew that he had really got himself a prize

FLEEING JERUSALEM

2 Kings 25:1-26; Jeremiah 29:10; Ezekiel 1:1-3; 8:1-18

Ten years showed since the king of Babylon took the smartest Israelites with him
Then God showed the prophet Ezekiel temples and the actions there were grim
It showed the image of creatures that were painted on the temple walls
Then God showed the people worshiping every painting with their happy calls
That showed since they thought God was gone and lot's of problems plagued the land
So God showed Ezekiel that they'd pay if idol worship kept at hand
Then three years passed which showed those prophecies to really be the truth
And God showed the Israelites at war which broke king Nebuchadnezzar's tooth
That showed the walls of Babylon as every one was torn right down
Then God showed the city burn which came to leave it as an empty town
But some of the Israelites were good which showed a few fine people stay
Then God showed them a man named Gedaliah who would lead the way
But that showed a problem when some Israelites walked in to kill their lead
And God showed the Babylonians who would come to punish them at speed
So they showed the path to Egypt and made Jeremiah come with fears
And God showed them that Israel was desolate for many years

THE MEN WHO WOULDN'T BOW

Exodus 20:3; Daniel 3:1-30

The king of Babylon brought all his people in as one to meet
Then he tended to the furnace as he filled it up with wood and heat
That followed with the king unveiling statues that were made of gold
Then he said that they would worship them at any time that they were told
And the king told them that music would be played to tell when it was time
Then horns and harps with other types of instruments began to chime
That showed the king three men who wouldn't bow down to the idols there
And they wouldn't cause the lord was one and only to deserve their prayer
It made the king feel angry and he pulled the army men right in
Then they tied them up and threw them in the furnace for their act of sin
That brought the king a shock as they untied themselves and walked through flames
So he knew that they were servants of the lord and called them by their names
Then the king said that the lord had saved their lives since they were loyal men
And he knew that they deserved to live each day inside his golden den

DANIEL IN THE LION'S PIT

Daniel 5:1-31; Daniel 6:1-28

The new king Belshazzar put on a feast with lot's of people there
Then two hands appeared and found the wall to write some letters in the air
So king Belshazzar brought wise men in to read the letters on the wall
Then they couldn't so he found the former chief of wise men they could call
That brought king Belshazzar his Daniel who read that they had all done wrong
Then they knew that they should not have given idols every worship song
It told king Belshazzar that Medes and Persians would take on the land
Then the armies of Medes and Persians killed him when they came to take their stand
That brought king Darius who then made Daniel chief of ruler to the throne
Then royal folks were jelous and much more than they had ever known
So they told king Darius that there should be another rule for thirty days
Then the rule was that no one would worship God and give the king their praise
But Daniel loved the lord and he was thrown in to the lion's pit
Then king Darius went to find him and he wasn't eaten up a bit
It told him that an angel came since Daniel always did things right
Then king Darius threw the other men in to the lion's pit that night

LEAVING BABYLON

Isaiah 44:28; 45:1-4; Ezra 1:1-11 Ezra chapters 2 to 8

Two years passed since the Medes and Persians captured Babylon which made them grieve
Then the king said building temples in Jerusalem should make them leave
So they took off as they walked for months with presents that were made of gold
But people passed by them and claimed that it was not what they were told
That brought Jerusalem a law against the temple building there
So they worked for months to build a brand new city with a lot of care
Then seventeen years passed till prophets said to build the temple up
That brought Jerusalem a place to put each jewel and golden cup
But after months a Persian official doubted that they had that right
So a letter passed through Babylon which put permission in to sight
Then after years Jerusalem looked old and people got so poor
That news went on to Ezra and in month's he found the kingdom's door
So the king in Babylon passed gifts on to Ezra in a big old crowd
But he feared that robbers plagued Jerusalem and started praying loud
Then they walked for months and still kept safe with all their gold and silver things
It got them passed which shows the strength that having God's faith always brings

NEHEMIAH BUILDS THE WALLS OF JERUSALEM

Nehemiah chapters 1 to 6

Nehemiah served the king of Shushan wine so no one poisoned it
The job was made important as the king enjoyed his wine each bit
Then Nehemiah had his brother and some men come visit him
That told him that they lived inside Jerusalem where times were grim
So Nehemiah felt sad and he asked the king if he could go
Then the sad men took him from the king to help the holy city grow
It told dear Nehemiah that they hadn't rebuilt walls that fell
So then without rebuilt walls invasions came to throw them down each well
But Nehemiah knew that they weren't built cause people there were poor
And he knew that he would have to help the people there a whole lot more
Then Nehemiah helped groups build as enemies saw workers there
That gave the enemies their plans to kill the workers without care
So Nehemiah got them spears and also handed them some swords
It handed them a lot of strength which made them feel like they were lords
That made them brave as Nehemiah built for fifty two long days
Then walls were built cause Israelites were brave from giving God their praise

Printed in the United States
By Bookmasters